HANDS-ON GEOLOGY

Get Hands-On with Rocks and Minerals!

Real geology experiments to try on your rock collection. With a rock ID chart!

PowerKiDS press

New York

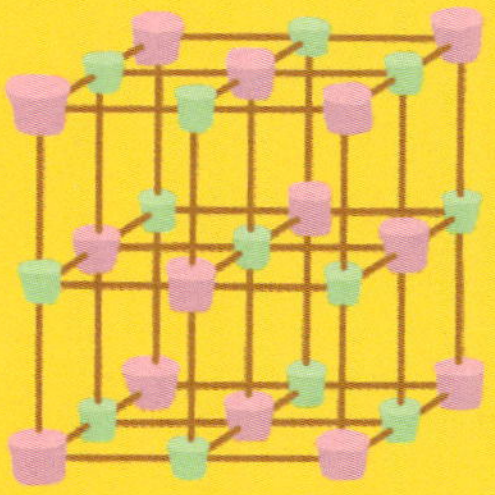

Published in 2022 by Rosen Publishing
29 East 21st Street, New York, NY 10010

Produced for Rosen Publishing by Alix Wood Books
Designed and Illustrated by Alix Wood
Editor: Eloise Macgregor
Consultant: Kate Spencer, Professor of Environmental Geochemistry

Cataloging-in-Publication Data
Names: Wood, Alix.
Title: Get hands-on with rocks and minerals! / Alix Wood.
Description: New York : PowerKids Press, 2022. | Series: Hands-on geology | Includes glossary and index.
Identifiers: ISBN 9781725331273 (pbk.) | ISBN 9781725331297 (library bound) | ISBN 9781725331280 (6 pack) | ISBN 9781725331303 (ebook)
Subjects: LCSH: Rocks--Juvenile literature. | Minerals--Juvenile literature. | Petrology--Juvenile literature.
Classification: LCC QE432.2 W66 2022 | DDC 552--dc23

Photo credits:
Cover, 1, 3, 4, 5, 8 top, 10, 12 top, 14, 15, 16, 17, 18, 20, 22, 24 top left, 25 top © AdobeStock Images; 8 bottom © Hans-Joachim Engelhardt; 10 bottom © James St. John; 13 metallic © JJ Harrison, glassy © Didier Descouens, resinous © Hannes Grobe, greasy © Ra'ike, pearly © Luis Miguel Bugallo Sánchez, brilliant © Robert M. Lavinsky, dull © Karla Panchuk; 24 top right © Alexander Van Driessche; 24 middle © Robert M. Lavinsky; 24 bottom © Malopolska's Virtual Museums Project

Printed in the United States of America

CPSIA Compliance Information: Batch #CSPK22. For Further Information contact Rosen Publishing, New York, New York at 1-800-237-9932.

Contents

What Exactly Is Rock?

Our planet, Earth, is made up of many layers. Rocks are the dry, solid material that makes up the outer layer of Earth, known as Earth's **crust**. If you go outside and look around, you are pretty sure to find some rock. Anything from a huge boulder to a grain of sand can be described as rock.

Broken rock, sand, and soil lie on the surface of Earth's crust. The lower part of the crust is solid rock. Underneath Earth's crust is a layer called the **mantle**. The mantle is mainly solid rock, with areas where the rock has melted from the extreme heat of Earth's **core**. As you head further toward the center of Earth, scientists believe the outer core is mainly liquid iron. The outer core surrounds a solid, mainly iron inner core.

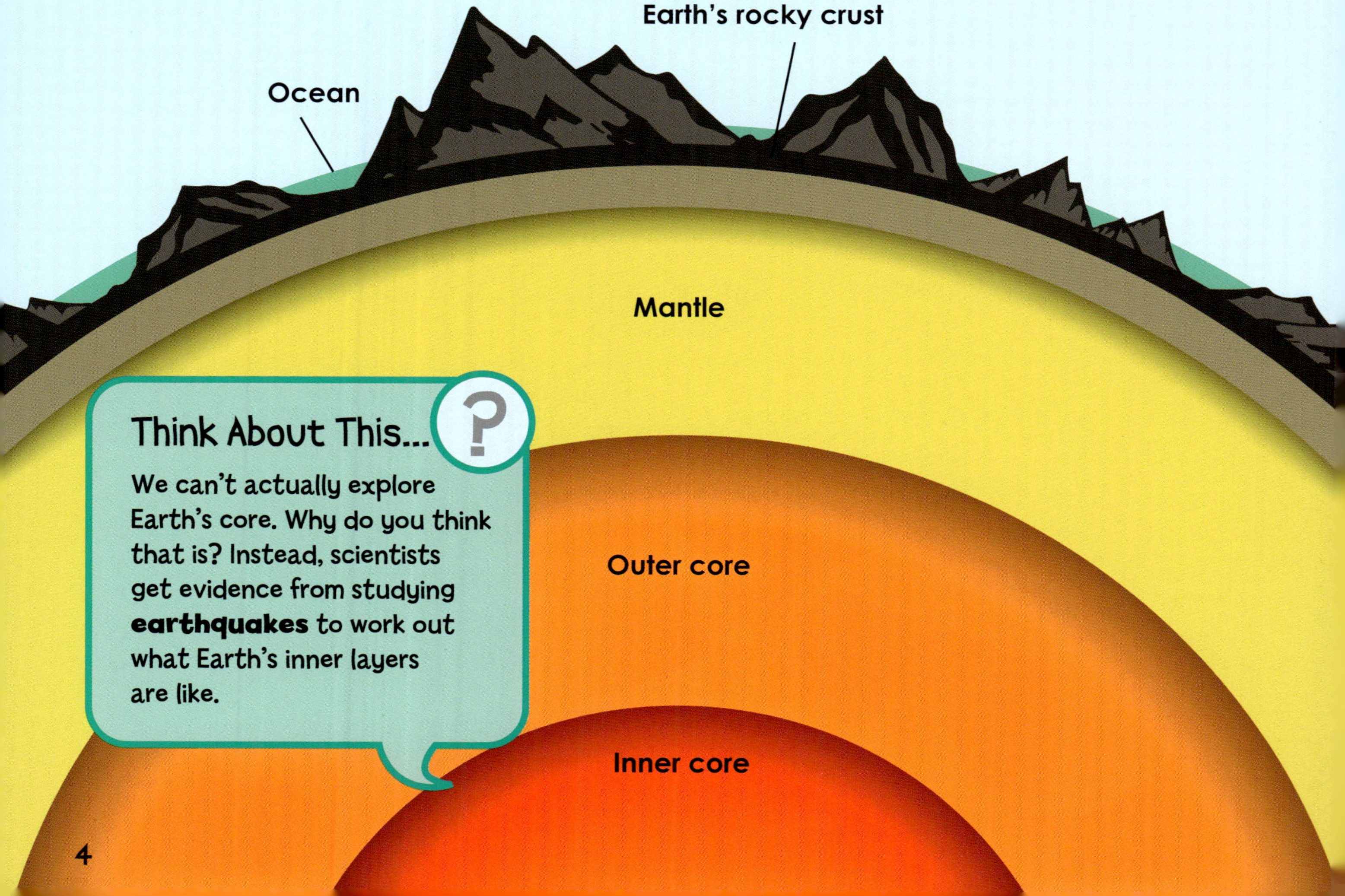

Think About This...

We can't actually explore Earth's core. Why do you think that is? Instead, scientists get evidence from studying earthquakes to work out what Earth's inner layers are like.

Why Study Rocks?

Rock are fascinating. They have been around since Earth was formed. The study of rocks is called **geology**. People who study rocks are called geologists. Rocks give us clues about what Earth was like long before people lived on the planet. Studying an area's rocks can tell geologists if there was once a lake or **volcano** there, if it was under the sea or part of a mountain range, and even what the temperatures were like.

Studying rocks helps geologists learn about volcanoes and earthquakes and predict where they might happen in the future. Fossils found in rocks give information about plants and animals that existed long ago. Studying an area's rocks can help find useful resources such as gold, jewels, or oil.

HANDS-ON Go Rock Collecting

You Will Need:

- a bag or backpack to carry your rocks home

You May Want:

- gloves
- a rock hammer or pick
- eye protection
- a magnifying glass or hand lens

ALWAYS wear eye protection when using a rock hammer. Small pieces of flying rock can hit you.

You may already have a rock collection. If not, start hunting. If you tell people about your hobby, other collectors might give you some of their spare rocks. Search your yard and your neighborhood. See how many different rocks you can find.

Check you can take rocks from the area first. It can be illegal to remove rocks, particularly from beaches or streams. Why? Rocks and pebbles help protect coasts and riverbanks from erosion. If every visitor took one pebble, that may be enough to cause damage. Many creatures hide under rocks, too, so removing rocks may make them homeless.

What Are Rocks Made Of?

Rocks are made up of **minerals**. Minerals are **inorganic** substances. Inorganic means not coming from a plant or an animal. Minerals are not made by people, either. They are found naturally in the Earth. Each mineral is made of a particular mix of **elements**. **Atoms** in these elements are arranged in a particular way, forming structures known as **crystals**.

Think About This...

"In" or "im" at the beginning of a word often means "not." Organic means coming from an animal or plant, so inorganic means not coming from an animal or plant. Can you think of any other words like that, that start with "in" or "im"?

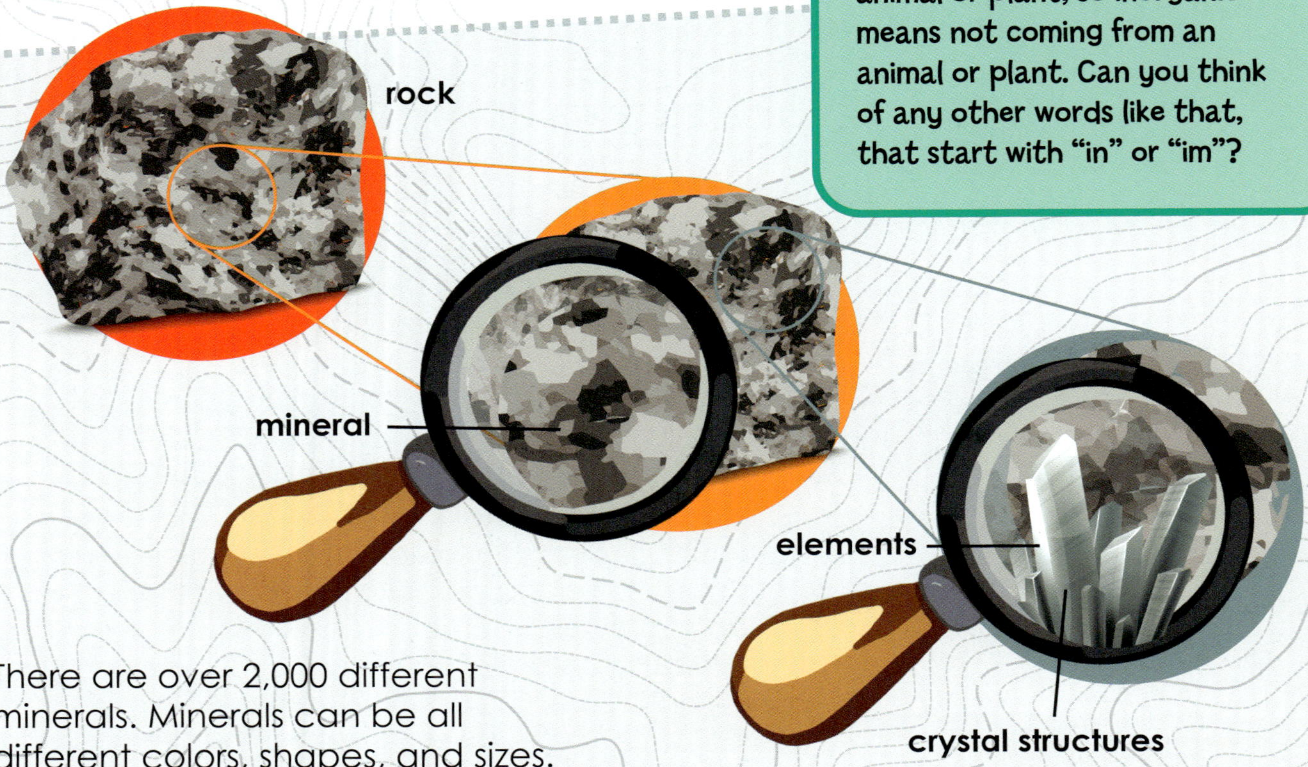

There are over 2,000 different minerals. Minerals can be all different colors, shapes, and sizes. Minerals are made from elements.

What Are Elements?

Elements are simple substances that cannot be broken down any further. For example, the mineral pyrite is made up of the elements iron and sulfur. You can break pyrite down into these two elements, but you cannot break those elements down further.

What Are Crystals?

Crystals form when a mineral's atoms fit together in a repeating pattern. Atoms are tiny particles that contain a mineral's chemical properties.

Kaolinite, a type of clay, has atoms that form sheets of crystals. The sheets slide over one another, making kaolinite feel slippery.

HANDS-ON Organize Your Rock Collection

You will need:
- some interesting rocks
- an old toothbrush
- paper and a pen
- some tape

Clean your **specimens** by carefully brushing away any dirt using a toothbrush. Sort your collection into things the rocks have in common, perhaps their size, color, texture, or how hard or shiny they are. Make a label for each specimen. Write down the place you found it and the date, and then tape the label onto each rock. If you know what type of rock it is, write that down too.

If you buy a rock, it's a good idea to keep any old labels. Rock collectors often note the name of the mine a rock was dug from, and the depth it was found at. They might write the price they paid for a rock and any history they have found out about it.

BE A ROCK DETECTIVE Make a Rock Identification Chart

You Will Need:
- pen, paper, and a ruler
- some masking tape

The Geology:

Geologists do **experiments** to identify the minerals in rocks they have found. Rocks can look very similar, but by carrying out a few simple tests geologists can work out what minerals the rocks contain. Try it!

How to Make Your Chart:

First, number your rock samples so you can identify them. Write each number on a piece of masking tape and stick a label onto each rock.

You will be conducting 13 experiments on your mystery rocks. Divide your paper into 14 columns. In the left hand column write your rock number. Write the experiment names along the top of your chart, starting in the second column. Now you are ready to record your results!

	Color	Hardness	Streak	Magnetism	Luster	Tranparency	Density	Texture	Scratch	Acidity	Cleavage	Absorbtion	Smell
Rock 1													
Rock 2													
Rock 3													

So Many Minerals!

There are thousands of different minerals found on Earth's surface and deep underground. Not everything that looks like a mineral is a mineral, and not every mineral looks like a rock. How do geologists decide what is a mineral and what isn't?

To be classed as a mineral, a substance must meet five requirements. It must be:

1. naturally occurring
2. inorganic
3. solid

And it must have:

4. a definite chemical composition
5. an ordered internal structure

"Naturally occurring" means it wasn't made by people, e.g. bronze is not a mineral. It is made when people mix tin and copper together.

"Inorganic" means not made by a living thing, e.g pearls are made by oysters so they cannot be minerals.

"Solid" means not a liquid or a gas at standard temperature and pressure. Water is not a mineral, but ice is.

"Definite chemical composition" means the mineral is always made in the same way, e.g. halite always has an equal number of atoms of the elements sodium and chlorine.

"Ordered internal structure" means its atoms are in a structured pattern, often seen in the shape of a mineral's crystals. Halite's sodium and chlorine atoms are arranged in a cube pattern. Its crystals are cube-shaped.

halite crystal

Think About This...

Do you know what common household substance is made from halite? You probably use it every day! Clue: halite is also known as rock salt.

EXPERIMENT ONE
Identify Minerals by Their Hardness

You Will Need:

- a copper coin (some copper coins are not pure copper. A pre-1982 U.S. penny is best)
- a steel nail
- some quartz if you have any

How to Test Your Rocks:

Try to scratch a specimen with your fingernail. Is the rock soft enough for your fingernail to leave a mark? If it is, look at the Mohs scale on the right. You'll see your rock might be talc or gypsum. If there was no mark, try scratching your specimen with a copper penny, and then a steel nail.

Scratching rock can create a powder that looks like a scratch. Rub any powder away. Can you still see a scratch?

If you are certain what a rock in your collection is, try scratching your specimen with that rock. If it leaves a mark, your specimen is softer on the scale. If it doesn't, it's harder.

The Geology:

Geologist Friedrich Mohs made a test to help identify minerals based on how hard or soft they are. Hard minerals will leave a scratch mark on softer ones. The Mohs scale is a list of ten minerals, from softest to hardest.

1. Talc
2. Gypsum
3. Calcite
4. Fluorite
5. Apatite
6. Orthoclase Feldspar
7. Quartz
8. Topaz
9. Corundum
10. Diamond

A fingernail is 2.5 on the Mohs scale. A copper coin is 3.5, and a steel nail is 5.5. So, if you can scratch a rock with a coin but not your fingernail, the rock is between 2.5 and 3.5.

Enter your results onto your identification chart. Knowing the hardness of a mineral may not be enough to identify it on its own, but it will help you narrow down what your rock is.

Metal Rocks

Around 99 percent of the minerals that make up Earth's crust are made from just eight elements. The elements are oxygen, silicon, aluminum, iron, calcium, sodium, potassium, and magnesium. Six of these elements are metals. The only nonmetal is oxygen. Silicon is a metalloid, meaning it has properties that both metals and nonmetals have. Other metals such as copper, silver, and gold can be found in rocks too.

EXPERIMENT TWO
Is Your Rock Magnetic?

You Will Need:

- a selection of rocks
- a magnet
- a compass

How to Test for Magnetism:

Will the magnet stick to your rock? If not, hold it lightly between your thumb and index finger. Hold it near the rock. Can you feel a slight pull? Pass the rock slowly around a compass placed flat on a table. Does the compass needle move?

Think About This...

When a breakfast cereal says it contains minerals such as iron, does that mean we eat metal? Mix a cereal high in iron with water. Spoon the mush into a ziplock bag. If you move a neodymium magnet over the bag, eventually you might see a cluster of iron flecks following the magnet!

The Geology:

Iron is magnetic, and is a common element in most surface rocks. Iron will stick to a magnet and move a compass needle. Minerals containing a lot of iron can be magnetic. Magnetite and maghemite are strongly magnetic. Other minerals such as chromite, siderite, and ilmenite are slightly magnetic.

There are over 70 different metal chemical elements. Rocks that are rich in metals are called **ores**. Ores must be processed to get the metal out. The ore is crushed into small pieces and then cleaned. Then the ore is heated until the elements separate and liquid metal flows out. This process is called **smelting**. Sometimes people use electricity and chemicals to separate metal from ore. We also might mix metals together with other metals or nonmetals to produce new metals called **alloys**. Steel is an alloy of iron and carbon. Bronze is an alloy of copper and tin.

One way to identify if you have metal elements in your rock sample is to perform a streak test. Rubbing the rock along an unglazed tile or paving slab will leave a streak mark. The color of this mark can help identify minerals in the rock. You would think a rock would leave a streak that is the same color as the rock itself. However, the surface of a rock can react with air, giving it a different color than the minerals within.

EXPERIMENT THREE
Sort Rocks Using a Streak Test

You Will Need:

- a selection of rocks
- a paving slab or an unglazed tile

The Geology:

Rocks don't always make the mark you expect. Pyrite and gold look really alike, but pyrite (known as fool's gold) makes a dark streak, whereas gold will make a gold-colored mark. Doing a streak test is a good way to easily tell them apart.

How to Do a Streak Test:

A streak test shows what color a rock would be if it was ground into a powder. You can help identify minerals by what color mark they make. Some minerals make quite distinctive marks. To do a streak test, take a clean rock and drag it very firmly across an unglazed tile or slab.

Mark Color	Possible Mineral
metallic red	copper
black	magnetite
silver white	silver
white to gray	platinum
green	malachite
brown	hematite (iron oxide)

Rocks Can Be See-Through, Shiny, and They Can Even Glow!

The way a mineral reflects light is known as **luster**. Some rocks are shiny like metal, others are dull. Some rocks are completely see-through too. The amount of light that can shine through a rock is known as a rock's **transparency**. The luster and transparency of a rock can help give you an idea what minerals it is made from.

Some minerals glow under ultraviolet light. Energy from the ultraviolet light reacts with chemicals in the mineral and causes it to glow. This glow is known as **fluorescence**. If a mineral emits enough energy, it may still glow after the ultraviolet light is turned off. That effect is known as **phosphorescence**.

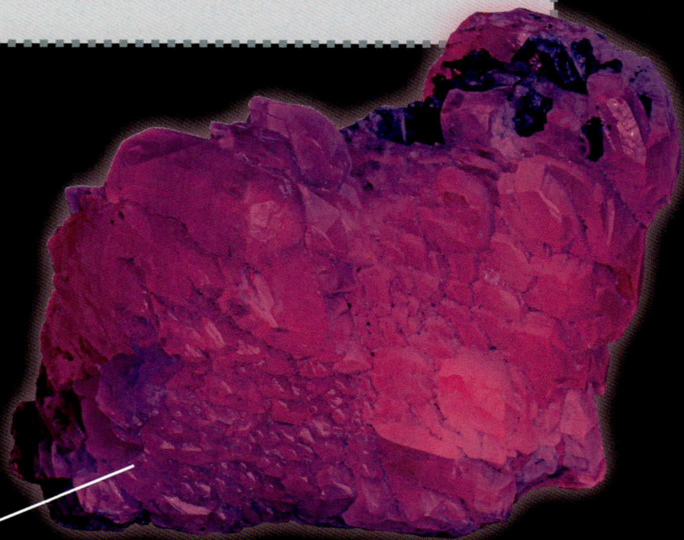

calcite fluorescence under ultraviolet light

HANDS-ON Can You Make a Rock Glow?

You Will Need:

- two rocks containing quartz
- eye protection
- a pair of pliers
- a dark room

A Native American tribe from Colorado filled buffalo hide rattles with quartz crystals. When the rattles were shaken at night the quartz crystals produced flashes of light!

IMPORTANT - Wear eye protection, as rock chips could fly into your face. Make sure the quartz is dry. Don't use your favorite crystals for this experiment as you will damage them. Most gravel has enough quartz in it for this experiment. In a dark room, firmly rub the two pieces of quartz together. You may see flashes of light. Now try striking one piece of quartz with the other. You should see small sparks. Try crushing a piece of quartz using pliers. You need a lot of pressure, but you may see the quartz glow.

What's happening? Squeezing the quartz crystals generates a tiny electric circuit. Light that is produced like this, by pressure or friction, is called **triboluminescence**.

EXPERIMENT FOUR
Luster and Transparency Tests

You Will Need:

- a desk lamp or strong daylight
- a magnifying glass
- a selection of minerals

How to Test for Luster:

Look at the surface of your mineral using a magnifying glass. Which of the words below best describes your mineral? Write the chosen word in the luster column in your table.

metallic - shines like metal and strongly reflects light

glassy - bright with a glassy shine

resinous - like tree sap or honey

greasy - a dull sheen, as if it was coated with oil

pearly - a whitish shimmer a little like a pearl

silky- a sheen like silk material

brilliant - a brilliant shine like a diamond

dull - no shine

Testing for Transparency

Hold your mineral up to the light. A mineral's transparency is how much light can pass through it. Choose a thin section, perhaps an edge or a corner, and look through the mineral toward your light source. Make a note in your table describing each mineral's transparency.

opaque

no light is passing through the mineral

translucent

light is passing through the mineral but images are not clear

transparent

light is passing through the mineral and images are clear

The Geology:

Many minerals are transparent or translucent. Mica is so transparent it was used in windows! Gypsum is translucent and can have a pearly, glassy, greasy, or silky luster. Gold is opaque. Minerals with a metallic luster are always opaque.

Beautiful Gemstones

turquoise

emerald

Gemstones are minerals or rocks that have been cut, shaped, and polished. They are collected and used in jewelry. Emeralds, rubies, and sapphires are types of gemstones. Any attractive crystal can be cut into a gem. Most gemstones are made from naturally occurring crystals, but some organic materials such as amber and pearls are classed as gems, too. Gems are valued for their size, beauty, and how rare they are.

Some minerals produce more than one type of gem. Pure corundum is colorless. If corundum contains chromium it becomes a red ruby. If it contains titanium it becomes a blue sapphire. The best sapphires are colored by both titanium and iron.

a blue sapphire and red ruby

Quartz can produce gems of many colors – purple quartz is amethyst, yellow is citrine, brown is smoky quartz, and pink is rose quartz. Stripy agate and tiger eye are also quartz.

tiger eye

amethyst quartz

Metal elements give most gems their color. Chromium gives a ruby its deep red and gives emeralds their brilliant green. Iron gives the red, blue, and yellow colors to garnet, sapphire, and peridot. Copper gives the blue and green color to turquoise and malachite.

malachite

A diamond is a unique gem as it is made of just one chemical – carbon. Diamond is the hardest natural substance on Earth. The only thing that will cut a diamond is another diamond! Diamonds vary in color. Rare red and colorless are the most valuable.

Diamonds form between 75 and 120 miles (120 and 200 kms) below Earth's crust. Over millions of years, extreme heat and pressure cause the carbon atoms to crystallize, forming diamonds. Volcanic eruptions then bring the diamonds to the surface.

Think About This...

Graphite, used in pencil lead, is also made of carbon atoms. Why is diamond the hardest mineral while graphite is one of the softest? Could it be how the carbon atoms are arranged?

The flashes of color in a diamond are known as "fire."

HANDS-ON How to Polish Your Rocks

You Will Need:

- soft to medium-hard rocks
- fine sandpaper
- a tin or plastic container with a tight-fitting lid
- water
- coarse sand or grit
- cooking oil or car wax
- a scrap of fabric
- some patience!

Half-fill your container with coarse sand or grit. Add water until the container is two-thirds full. Place some rocks in the container that are similar in hardness. Tightly fit the lid. Now shake and roll the container for as long and often as you can, over several days. It can take weeks to make hard rocks smooth!

To make your rocks really smooth, sand them using a fine grain sandpaper. Wet the paper and gently sand each rock. Wipe away any dust.

Finally, dab some car wax or cooking oil onto a scrap of fabric. Gently polish the wax or oil into the stones. They should now look amazingly shiny!

Three Main Types of Rock

Geologists sort rocks into three main groups; **igneous**, **metamorphic**, and **sedimentary**.

- Igneous rocks form when molten rock deep within Earth rises and cools.
- Metamorphic rocks have been changed by great heat and pressure under Earth's surface.
- Sedimentary rocks are made when sand, shells, and pebbles are carried by water, ice, or the wind. Known as sediment, this mixture settles by lakes, oceans, and deserts. Over millions of years it forms a layer of rock.

Think About This...

"Metamorphosis" means "change" in Greek. In Latin. "ignius" means "fire" and "sedere" means "to settle." If you can remember this, it may help you remember how each type of rock is formed.

Sedimentary Rock

When wind and water **erode** rock, the crumbling pieces of rock end up in streams and rivers that flow down the mountains. The pieces of rock and other matter are compressed and form sediment.

Dead animals and plants in the sediment can become preserved as fossils in the layers of sedimentary rock as it is compressed.

To tell if a rock sample is sedimentary, first see if you can find any fossils in it. Although other rock types can contain fossils, it is really very rare. Sedimentary rock is usually fairly soft and crumbly. You can sometimes see pebbles or stones cemented together in the rock. As sedimentary rock is formed in layers, you might see layers of different colors in the rock sample or at the place you found it.

fossils

limestone

conglomerate

sandstone

EXPERIMENT FIVE
Identify Rocks with an Acid Test

You Will Need:

- lemon juice or vinegar
- a glass
- some rock specimens
- magnifying glass
- eye protection

How to Do an Acid Test:

Wear eye protection. You don't want acid fizzing into your eyes. Pour half a cup of lemon juice or vinegar into a glass. Add your rock specimen.

Observe what happens using a magnifying glass. The rock may start to react with the liquid. It may fizz and create small bubbles.

The Geology:

Lemon juice and vinegar are acids. Acid dissolves carbonate found in some rocks. The reaction releases carbon dioxide gas in the form of small bubbles. If your rock fizzes, it contains carbonate.

Your rock could be limestone, chalk, or dolomite, which are sedimentary rocks. It could be marble, a metamorphic rock made when limestone is exposed to heat and pressure. It could be calcite or aragonite, which are found in all three types of rock.

Beware–some rocks, such as sandstone, have holes that trap pockets of air. The escaping air can appear to fizz, but sandstone does not contain carbonate. Double-check the reaction by scratching some rock onto a plate and spooning the acid onto the powder.

Igneous Rock

Earth is made mostly of a large mass of igneous rock with a very thin layer of sedimentary rock on top. While sedimentary rocks are produced by processes at Earth's surface, both igneous and metamorphic rocks are formed deep under the ground.

Think About This...

Devils Tower, Wyoming, is an example of igneous rock. Created underground by a volcano around 50 million years ago, the hot magma cooled, creating this amazing rock with hexagonal-shaped columns. Originally formed underground, why do you think Devils Tower is now aboveground?

How can you tell if you have igneous rocks in your rock collection? Examine your specimens. What do you see?

Large crystals? Igneous rocks can be formed when molten magma cools deep inside Earth. The rocks gradually work their way to the surface. Known as **intrusive**, or **plutonic**, igneous rock, the slow cooling means large crystals get trapped in the rock. An example of this type of rock is granite.

granite

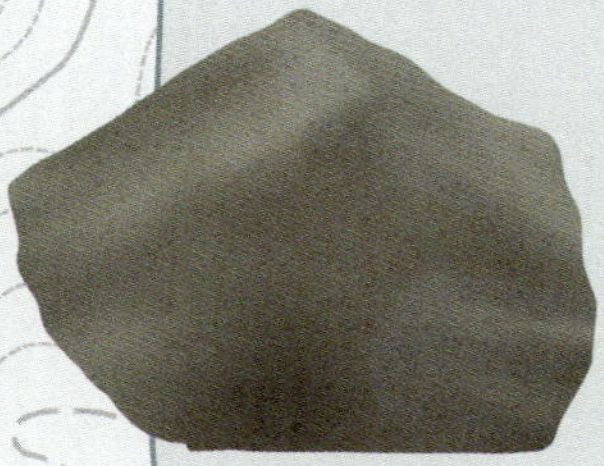
basalt

Glassy or fine texture? Igneous rocks also form when magma erupts from volcanoes. The hot **lava** cools to form **extrusive**, or **volcanic**, igneous rock. The lava cools quickly, so mineral crystals don't have time to grow. These igneous rocks have a fine texture, like basalt, or a glassy texture, like obsidian.

obsidian

scoria

Holes? Hot gas bubbles can get trapped in lava, leaving tiny holes in the rock. Pumice and scoria are good examples of this type of igneous rock.

EXPERIMENT SIX
Measuring Specific Gravity

Specific gravity is a measurement of the **density** of something. To work out what a specimen's specific gravity is, we need to measure the density of the sample, and then compare that to the density of an equal volume of water. How? Try making your own Jolly balance.

You Will Need:

- a stick
- books
- string
- a spring from a ballpoint pen
- paper fastener
- a ruler
- a large jar half full of water
- rocks smaller than half the jar

How to Test Your Rocks:

Rest a stick across two piles of books of equal height. Hook or tie one end of the spring to the stick. Tie one end of a piece of string to the rock sample. Tie the other end to the bottom of the spring. Clip an opened paper fastener on the string. Secure a ruler next to your dangling rock. Record where the paper clip pointer points to on your ruler. Lift the rock and place the jar of water under it. Lower the rock into the jar. Record the paper clip pointer reading again.

The Geology:

Most minerals Earth's crust have very similar densities, of around 2.6 to 3.0 grams per cubic cm. Metallic samples are usually the densest. Some elements such as iridium and platinum can have densities as high as 20! Rocks can have a range of densities, as different specimens may contain different amounts of each mineral. Granite can be between 20 and 60 percent quartz.

Rock	Specific Gravity
Sandstone	2.2–2.8
Granite	2.6-2.7
Basalt	2.8-3.0
Iron Ore	4.5-5.3
Lead Ore	7.5

To calculate the specific gravity of your rock, divide the first reading by the first reading minus the second reading:

$$\frac{\text{Weight of Mineral in Air [20]}}{\text{Weight of Mineral in Air [20] - Weight of Mineral in Water [15]}}\ (20-15 = 5)$$

20 divided by 5 is 4, so the specific gravity is 4.

This metamorphic rock face in Japan was created when layers of sandstone and shale were heated and compressed to create this banded hornfel rock.

Metamorphic Rock

Metamorphic rock is formed from other rock that is changed by heat and pressure deep under the surface of Earth. Metamorphic rock originally could have been sedimentary or igneous rock, or older metamorphic rock. The heat and pressure rearranges the elements to form new minerals. The conditions underground have to be just right. Too much heat or pressure and the rock will melt, become magma, and form igneous rock instead.

Metamorphic rocks have what is known as parent rocks – that is, a rock that they were formed from. For instance, marble might be formed from limestone or dolomite. Slate is formed from shale or occasionally from basalt.

Think About This...

Metamorphic rocks can be made from sedimentary rocks that contain fossils. Metamorphic rocks rarely contain fossils though. Why do you think that might be?

Gneiss

Parent rocks:

shale

granite

Gneiss has banded layers of different minerals. Parent rocks can be shale, sandstone, feldspar, quartz, mica, or granite! It is often used for building and paving.

Marble

Parent rocks:

limestone

dolomite

Marble is a hard rock made of crystals. Impurities can color marble gray, black, red, green, pink, banded, and mottled! It is used for sculpture and building.

Slate

Parent rocks:

shale

basalt

Slate is formed at a lower pressure and temperature than many metamorphic rocks. It naturally splits into fine sheets, making it perfect for roof tiles.

EXPERIMENT SEVEN
Testing Cleavage and Fracture

How a rock or mineral breaks into pieces can give you a clue to what it is. If it breaks along flat surfaces, that is called **cleavage**. If it breaks and creates uneven surfaces, that is known as **fracture**.

You Will Need:

- minerals you are happy to break
- two towels
- a hard outdoor floor area
- a hammer
- eye protection
- gloves

adult help needed

How to Test Your Minerals:

To test your mineral samples, lay a towel on the ground on a hard surface. Place the sample on the towel. Cover the sample with the other towel. IMPORTANT - put on eye protection, as the towel may not catch all the flying pieces. Wear gloves, as fragments may be sharp.

Hit your covered sample with the hammer. Lift up the top towel and examine your pieces. Can you see a flat-edged shape? Then you are looking at cleavage. Or are there uneven fragments? Record the look and texture of the pieces on your mineral chart.

The Geology:

The mineral galena will break into perfect cubes. This is known as cleavage along three planes. Why three? Because parallel surfaces count as the same plane! Mica's cleavage is in one plane, as mica will break into thin sheets. The kind of cleavage a mineral has is because of its structure, not its original shape. A six-sided crystal will actually fracture, not create six flat surfaces!

Minerals that do not break into geometric shapes will fracture instead. Minerals can fracture into all kinds of irregular shapes. Some create bowl-shaped curves with sharp edges. Look at the fracture surfaces. Some are smooth, some are rough, and some can look like needles or splinters.

Think About This... ?

Early humans made tools and weapons from flint fragments. How do you think flint would fracture?

The Great Rock ReCycle

We know that metamorphic rocks change, but do you think an igneous rock will always be an igneous rock? Over time, all rocks actually change from one type to another. How? Forces inside Earth gradually move the underground igneous and metamorphic rocks to the surface. On the surface they get weathered and eroded. Other forces then compact them and sink them back down, where they are heated and pressed into sedimentary rock, or melted to form magma. In this way, all the minerals that make up Earth's rocks are constantly being recycled.

Think About This...

Earth is 4.6 billion years old. Most of its early crust has been recycled several times since the planet formed. However, in 2008, scientists found rock in northern Quebec, Canada, that has remained unchanged for 4.28 billion years!

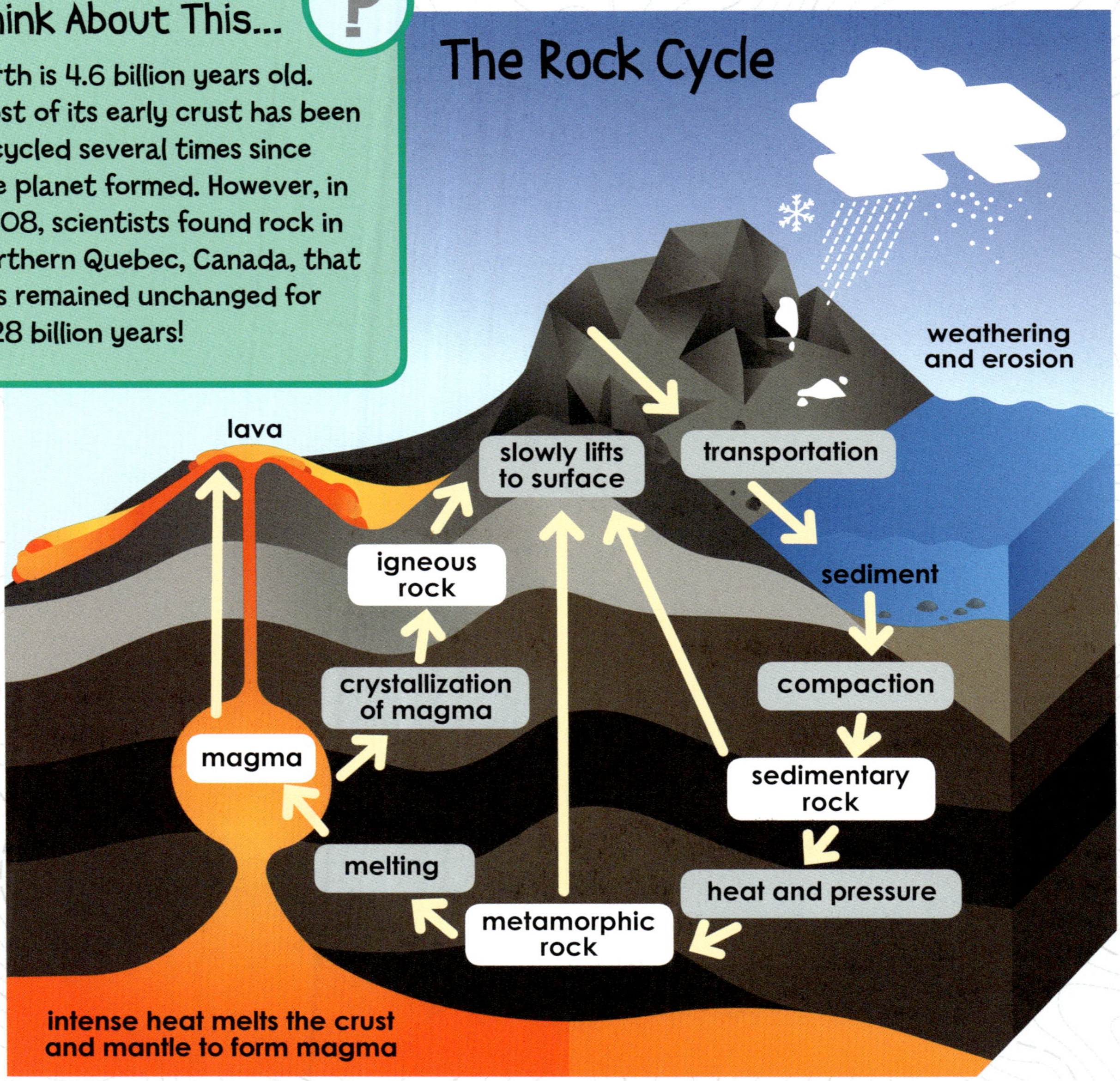

EXPERIMENT EIGHT
Bake a Chocolate Rock Cycle

You Will Need:

- white and dark chocolate
- a cheese grater
- a bowl
- a spoon
- aluminum foil
- a baking sheet
- an oven heated to 200°F (90°C)
- a bowl of hot water

adult help needed

The Geology:

The grater turned the chocolate "rock" into smaller pieces, just as rock is eroded and weathered in nature. Our sedimentary rock was made by pressure on the eroded chocolate. The force of being pressed into the mold and the heat of the oven created our metamorphic chocolate rock. Igneous rock was made when our melted chocolate "magma" cooled.

How to Make Them:

To mimic rock erosion, grate some white and dark chocolate into the same bowl. Ask an adult to help you, as graters are sharp. Divide the chocolate shavings into three equal portions.

To make your sedimentary rock, press one of the portions of grated chocolate together using the back of a spoon.

To make metamorphic rock, create a rock-shaped mold out of foil. Press the second portion of grated chocolate into the mold. Put the mold on a baking sheet. Put in the oven for a couple of minutes until the chocolate has melted. Leave to cool.

Now make your igneous rock. Ask an adult to help fill a cup with boiling water. Wrap the last portion of grated chocolate in some foil and carefully lower it into the water. After a few minutes, lift the foil out. Put it in the refrigerator to harden. Then unwrap your "rock."

Amazing Crystals

Crystals form when a liquid, such as magma, cools and hardens. The **molecules** in the liquid pull together in a repeating pattern, creating each crystal's shape. Crystals form beautiful, unique shapes. Snowflakes, diamonds, and table salt are examples of crystals. Crystals can also form when water evaporates from a chemical mixture. Salt crystals form when salt water evaporates.

These enormous gypsum crystals were found recently at a mine in Naica, Mexico.

Rocks' building blocks

A mineral's crystal structure is as important as the elements it contains. Graphite is the soft, dark material used in pencil lead. Diamond is a hard, often colorless, gemstone. These two minerals are very different, and yet they are both made from pure carbon.

They are different because they have completely different crystal structures. Graphite forms loosely bonded sheets that rub off as you draw with a pencil. Diamond forms a tightly stacked cubic crystal structure.

diamond

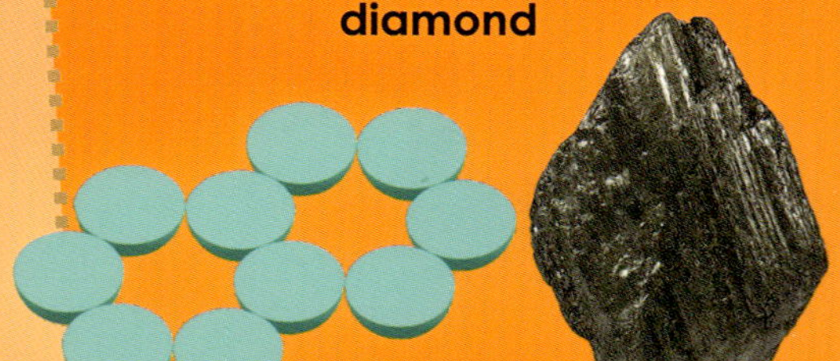

graphite

HANDS-ON Marshmallow Crystals

You Will Need:
- toothpicks
- marshmallows

halite

Halite, or rock salt, forms cube-shaped crystals. Try creating its crystal structure using marshmallows and toothpicks! Halite, like table salt, is made from sodium and chlorine. You could use different-colored marshmallows for each element.

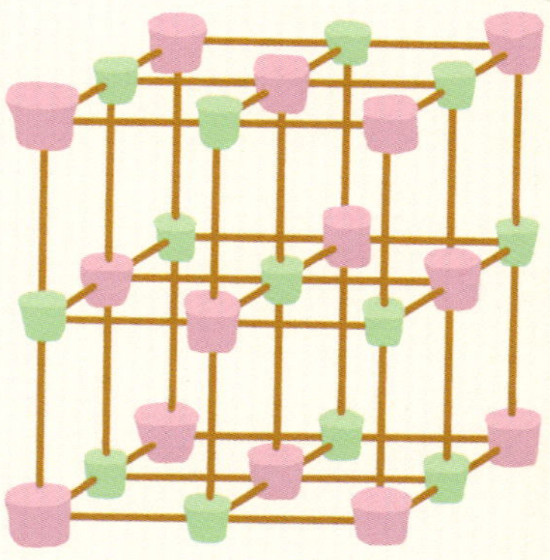

Geodes are round, ordinary-looking rocks with a hole inside lined with minerals. The outer rock is hard, allowing the geode to survive if the surrounding rock weathers away. Geodes can be lined with quartz or calcite crystals, colorful bands of agate, purple amethyst, and other beautiful minerals. You can buy geodes from rock stores to crack open yourself with a hammer!

EXPERIMENT NINE
Grow Your Own Crystal Geode

You Will Need:

adult help needed

- two low glasses
- boiling water
- food coloring
- alum powder (in the grocery store spice section)
- a measuring cup and spoon
- an egg

The Geology:

Rock geodes take thousands of years to form. This experiment speeds it up a little! As the warm alum solution cools, the particles of alum fall to the bottom and start to turn into crystals. Coating the shell with alum powder gives the particles a friendly surface to attach to. Your eggshell geode is created in the same way sedimentary rock is created. Particles in a liquid will settle against a barrier, whether that is the bottom of the ocean or the side of an eggshell!

How to Make Your Geode:

Gently crack an egg into a glass so the shell splits in half. Carefully peel off the membrane from inside one half. Rinse it and let it dry.

Ask an adult to pour one cup of boiling water into the other glass. Add four tablespoons of alum to the water and stir until the alum dissolves. Add a few drops of food coloring.

Sprinkle some alum powder inside the half eggshell. Submerge the shell, open side up, so it rests at the bottom of the alum solution.

After several hours, sparkling crystals should have formed inside your eggshell geode!

Some Very Unusual Rocks

There are some rocks which have unusual properties. Try some of the tests on this page and see if any of your collection absorb water, make you see double, or maybe just smell weird!

Viking sunstone

EXPERIMENT TEN
Do Rocks Absorb Water?

You Will Need:

- some rocks including pumice, chalk, or sandstone
- a measuring jug or beaker
- water
- a set of scales
- a pen and paper
- some foil

The Geology:

Rocks such as granite have grains that fit tightly together. They do not absorb water.

Rocks with rounded, loose grains, such as sandstone; or holes, such as pumice, will absorb water.

In some areas, water stored in layers of rock, known as aquifers, is pumped to the surface and used as drinking water.

How to Check Absorbancy:

Weigh your rock sample. Write down the result. Fill a measuring jug or beaker with enough water to cover the rock. Record the amount of water.

Carefully place your rock into the water. You don't want to splash any water out. Cover the jug with foil to prevent evaporation.

After a day, carefully take out the rock and weigh it. Measure how much water is in the jug. Write down both results.

If your rock weighs the same, and the water levels stayed the same, then your specimen probably isn't absorbent.

Think About This...

Did any of your rocks float? Why do you think that might happen?

HANDS-ON Identify by Smell!

You Will Need:

- any of the following: sulfur, pyrite, kaolinite, jet, or amber
- a needle

adult help needed

Some minerals and elements give off a distinctive odor. Sulfur and pyrite smell a little like when someone strikes a match. If you hit two pieces together, they smell like rotten eggs! If you smell garlic instead, put the rock down and wash your hands. You have found an arsenopyrite specimen, which contains the poison, arsenic!

Clay minerals such as kaolinite smell like fresh clay when damp.

If you have a jet or amber specimen that you don't mind poking a hole in, ask an adult to heat a needle and stick it in the specimen. Jet smells like burning tar and amber smells like burning pine sap. Jet and amber aren't actually minerals. Jet is compressed wood and amber is tree resin.

A type of calcite known as Iceland spar makes you see double! When light passes through the crystals, it is split into two rays. The two beams are bent by different amounts, causing a double image.

It is believed Viking navigators used the stone to help tell where the sun was on cloudy days. How? They marked a dot on the stone. If they looked through the stone they would see two dots. Looking through the stone, they moved it along the horizon. They saw two dots until the stone lined up directly under the sun. Then the rings of light that surround the sun, even under cloudy skies, would cause the second dot to disappear.

If you placed a specimen of Iceland spar on some typed text, you would see double!

Can You Identify Your Rocks?

Look at your experiment results and see if you can identify your rock samples using this chart. If you don't think your specimen is listed, ask an adult if they can help you try an internet search. Type in your results, such as "gray banded rock," "large grains," "white streak test," or "waxy luster" and you may find your rock that way.

Name	**Color**	**Hardness**	**Streak**
agate	all colors, multicolored, or banded	6.5-7	white
apatite	yellow, green, blue, brown	5	white
basalt	gray to black or brown	6	white - gray
calcite	mainly colorless or white	3	white
conglomerate	tan to brown	2-3	white
corundum	many colors or colorless	9	white
dolomite	white, gray, pink or brownish-white	3.5-4	white
feldspar	pink, white, gray, brown, blue	6-6.5	white
flint	gray, black, brown, red, white	6.5-7	white
fluorite	colorless or colored by impurities	4	white
galena	lead gray and silvery	2.5-2.7	lead gray
granite	red, pink, gray, or white	6-7	white
graphite	black to silver-gray	1-2	black
gypsum	colorless, white, gray, yellow, red, brown	2	white
halite	clear, white, red, or orange	2.5	white
hematite	black, silver gray or red to brown	5-6	red brown
limestone	white or almost white	3-4	white
magnetite	black or gray with a brown tint	5.5-6.5	black
malachite	bright, dark, or blackish-green	3.5-4	light green
marble	black, blue, brown, gray, pink, white	3-4	white
mica	colorless, transparent, or many colors	2-4	white/none
obsidian	deep black or blackish-green	5-6	white
olivine	olive, bright, or yellowish-green	6.5-7	none
pumice	usually white, cream, blue, or gray	6	white/green
pyrite	brassy yellow	6-6.5	green/black
quartz	colorless, transparent, or many colors	7	white
sandstone	gray, yellow, red, or white	6-7	white
scoria	dark brown, purple, or black	5-6	white
shale	usually gray	3	white
slate	gray, black, with blue, brown, green	3-4	brown
talc	Light to dark green, white, gray, colorless	1	white

Igneous, sedimentary, metamorphic?

- If your rock has layers- it is a metamorphic or sedimentary rock.
- Only sedimentary rocks, and very rarely metamorphic rocks, contain fossils.
- Only sedimentary rocks will have complete fossils.
- Sedimentary rocks' crystals are easily broken or scratched.
- Metamorphic rocks are usually brittle and lightweight, igneous rocks are dense and hard.

Luster	S. Gravity	Other properties
waxy	2.6	sharp fracture
glassy	3.2	six-sided crystals
dull	2.8-3	fine grain
glassy/pearly	2.7	reacts to acid test
dull	2.8	coarse grain with gravel lumps
glassy/brilliant	3.9-4.1	mostly see-through
glassy/pearly	2.8	might react to acid test
glassy	2.6-2.8	cleavage along two or three planes
waxy/dull	2.7	fractures with sharp edges
glassy	3.2	may be fluorescent
metallic	5.4	cleavage creates perfect cubes
mainly dull	2.7	dark mineral grains
metallic	1.8-2.3	has a greasy feel and smudges
glassy/silky	2.3-2.7	water-soluble, splits into thin sheets
dull/glassy	2.1-2.6	salty taste, cubic cleavage
metallic/dull	5.2-5.3	may easily break off into flakes
dull/pearly	2.3-2.7	fine grain, soluble in water and acid
metallic	5.2	strongly magnetic
brilliant/glassy/dull	3.6-4	forms green bands
dull/pearly	2.9	might react to acid test
pearly/glassy	2.8-3	splits into thin sheets
glassy	2.4	fractures with very sharp edges
glassy	3.2-4.4	found in many meteorites
dull	2.9	fine grains, holes, floats, absorbs water
metallic	4.9-5.2	can form different-shaped crystals
glassy/waxy/dull	2.6	some quartz crystals glow if pressed
dull	2.2-2.8	gritty, will absorb water
glassy/dull	1	features bubble-like holes
dull	2.6	fine grains, breaks into thin layers
dull	2.5	breaks into thin layers, rings if struck
waxy/pearly	2.6-2.8	very soft, scratched by a fingernail

Glossary

alloys a substance of two or more metals or a metal and nonmetal united usually by being melted together.

atoms the smallest particles of an element, having all the characteristics of that element.

cleavage the tendency for a rock or mineral to break along a flat surface.

core the central part of Earth.

crust the outer part of Earth.

crystals solid forms of a substance or mixture that have a regularly repeating internal arrangement of atoms and often external plane faces.

density the mass per unit volume.

earthquakes a shaking or trembling of a portion of Earth's surface.

elements fundamental substances that consist of atoms of only one kind and that cannot be separated into simpler substances.

erode to wear away by or as if by the action of water, wind, or glacial ice.

experiments procedures or operations carried out under controlled conditions in order to discover something.

extrusive formed by a volcano in a melted state or as volcanic ash.

fluorescence giving off radiation usually as visible light when exposed to radiation from another source.

fracture any separation in a rock, such as a joint or fault, that divides the rock into two or more pieces.

geodes stones having a cavity lined with crystals or mineral matter.

geology a science that deals with the history of Earth and its life, especially as recorded in rocks.

igneous formed by hardening of melted Earth.

inorganic composed of matter that does not come from plants or animals either alive or dead.

intrusive having been forced while melted into cavities or between layers.

lava melted rock coming from a volcano.

luster a shine or sheen especially from reflected light.

mantle the portion of Earth lying between the crust and the core.

metamorphic changed into a more compact form by the action of pressure, heat, and water.

minerals solid chemical compounds that occur naturally in the form of crystals.

molecules the simplest unit of a chemical substance, usually a group of two or more atoms.

opaque not letting light through.

ores minerals mined to obtain a substance they contain.

phosphorescence a light given off at low temperatures caused by the absorption of radiation and continuing for a time after these radiations have stopped.

plutonic relating to igneous rock formed by solidification at considerable depth beneath Earth's surface.

sedimentary formed by or from sediment.

smelting to melt metal, usually in order to separate it.

specimens a portion of material for use in testing or examination.

translucent not transparent, but clear enough to allow light to pass through.

transparency being transparent.

transparent being see-through.

triboluminescence the emission of light from a substance caused by rubbing.

volcanic relating to or produced by a volcano.

volcano a vent in Earth's crust from which melted or hot rock and steam come out.

Further Information

Museums and Places to Visit

Visit a museum. Many museums will have exhibits and information about local rocks and minerals.

Visit local rock shops. Enthusiasts love sharing their information.

Look for beginners' geology classes. If a college in your area teaches geology, it may have classes for young people.

Useful Websites

Try taking this National Geographic quiz on rocks and minerals.
https://kids.nationalgeographic.com/games/quizzes/quiz-whiz-rocks-minerals/

The Geological Society has plenty of information about rocks and the rock cycle.
https://www.geolsoc.org.uk/ks3/gsl/education/resources/rockcycle.html

Kids Love Rocks has plenty of information on crystals, rock types, and how to make a rock collection.
https://kidsloverocks.com/types-of-rock

Books to Read

Dennie, Devin. *My Book of Rocks and Minerals: Things to Find, Collect, and Treasure*. London, UK: DK Children, 2017.

Honovich, Nancy. *Ultimate Explorer Field Guide: Rocks and Minerals*. Washington, D.C.: National Geographic Kids, 2016.

Publisher's note to parents and teachers: Our editors have reviewed the websites listed here to make sure they're suitable for students. However, websites may change frequently. Please note that students should always be supervised when they access the internet.

Index